D1519878

Published by Gingko Press Inc.
5768 Paradise Drive, Suite J, Corte Madera, CA 94925
Phone (415) 924–9615, Fax (415) 924–9608
email gingko@linex.com

ISBN 3–92725–40–7

Excerpted from: *Albert Camus, a Biography*

Copyright © 1997 by Herbert R. Lottman

Book design by Julie von der Ropp
Printed in Germany

Albert Camus
in
New York

Herbert R. Lottman

Gingko Press
Corte Madera, California
1997

A Word from the Author

If it had not actually taken place I should have been tempted, when writing a biography of Albert Camus, to invent his visit to my birthplace city. The timing of the actual event—for it did happen—is touched with irony. By then Camus was a hero in Paris, a still young and brilliant author of eminently readable yet challenging works, perhaps more widely known as editor-in-chief of *Combat*, a daily newspaper born of the wartime Resistance. Now, as front-page editorialist of a paper and a movement pledged to change France, Albert Camus was seen as a moral guide for the postwar.

He was also a very likeable hero, looking even younger than his years, dapper in his Humphrey Bogart raincoat (looking very much a Bogart clone, and enjoying the notion when told so). He might be spotted in the literary heart of the Left Bank, at one or another sidewalk cafe of Place Saint-Germain-des-Prés, late evenings at a cabaret or jazz cellar. The popular press knew a good story when it saw one. The very fact that Camus had been born and grew up in far-off French Algeria , then had spent his first French years in a remote province, made his sudden appearance among the literary warhorses of the French capital more magical still.

Yet—this is the irony—he was all but unknown on foreign shores—our shores for example. *The Stranger*, his first influential novel, was to be published only during his American visit. University specialists knew something about him, and some were already great admirers, as were a handful of Francophile journalists. Still, his relative obscurity, and his total accessibility, added intensity to his brief stay—for Camus as well as for some fortunate enough to meet him then, and for us as we reach back to the past to re-create those days.

Paris 1997   Herbert R. Lottman

Albert Camus
in
New York

I loved New York, with that powerful love that at times leaves you full of uncertainty and abhorrence: there are times when one needs an exile.

"Pluies de New York"

"I am not displeased," Camus wrote to his aging Belcourt elementary-school teacher Louis Germain, "to abandon for a while this Parisian life which wears down your nerves and dries up your heart."[1]

A representative figure of the French resistance, a young cultural and social personality of eminence, Camus was a logical candidate for a mission to the United States, particularly to its universities, under French Government sponsorship. His tour was sponsored by the Cultural Relations Section of the French Ministry of Foreign Affairs; while in the United States he would be on official business for the Provisional Government of the French Republic (but with no particular obligations). Such trips were at once good public relations for the dispatching government and a reward—a paid vacation—for eminent citizens.

Camus sailed from Le Havre on the *Oregon*, which was being operated by the French Line as a cargo and passenger liner. The fact that it was a freighter came as a surprise to Camus, especially when he discovered that all its passengers could fit into a small dining room. Conditions were virtually those of wartime austerity (France was out of the war but it had lost the war, and the armistice had been signed less than a year ago). Camus shared a cabin with three other men, one of whom was a doctor and a new friend.

Dr. Pierre Rubé, a psychiatrist by training, had been an army doctor at the outbreak of the war, assigned to a hospital train. He participated in the June 1940 débacle, and after unsuccessful attempts to get out of France, during which he joined an underground intelligence network in Montpellier, he managed to escape over the Pyrenees with a Spanish Republican guide. Arrested in Barcelona, he was interned in a camp for six months, then sent to North Africa, where he fought with the Leclerc division, following it to the battlefields of Normandy, Paris, Strasbourg, taking part in the liberation of the Dachau concentration camp. He returned to Paris sick at heart, the very sight of Nazi collaborators making him nauseated. A friend got him a mission to the United States to study psychiatric teamwork, a speciality which interested him. While applying for the necessary travel documents he met Camus, who was of course going through the same procedures. Rubé had just seen Camus' *Caligula* at the Hébertot theater, and he had been moved by it. He introduced himself and expressed his admiration for the play. It was snowing, and they had to go to the American Consulate for their visas. Camus offered to drive Rubé there in his black Citroën.

On board the *Oregon* they found not only accommodations but amusement facilities spare;

there were no movies or other group entertainment. But Camus was in excellent humor, joking with everyone, flirting with the younger women. Rubé noticed one characteristic of his new friend, an aspect of Mediterranean man: He always took it for granted that he, and not a woman, would go through a door first.

They could take showers whenever they wanted to, but there was a French consular official sharing their tiny cabin who never did, and the Camus-Rubé team wondered how they could oblige him to bathe. Finally Rubé had an idea. He enlisted the help of their steward, with a tip, so the steward knocked at the door of their cabin the next morning to announce: "Monsieur the Consul, your shower is ready." The steward was carrying soap and a towel, and the strategy worked.[2]

When their ship docked in New York on March 25, 1946 (it had been anchored in the middle of the Hudson since the previous evening), foreign passengers were interrogated by Immigration inspectors. They were asked, among other things, whether they had ever been members of the Communist Party or had friends who had been members, and Camus apparently refused to reply to either question. Arriving passengers were questioned individually, and Rubé and the others in their group waited outside the examination room for Camus to come out, but he did not. An hour passed, then another half hour, and finally one of the group returned to find out what had happened. He was informed by an angry Camus that he had Communist friends but wouldn't name them. Finally the others went on to the French Cultural Services to tell the people there what had happened, and an emissary was sent to help get Camus out.[2]

Camus himself reported having been held up by Immigration inspectors, who seemed to have mysterious sources of information—but who later apologized for the delay.[3]

As it happened, the head of French Cultural Services in New York at the time was the anthropologist Claude Lévi-Strauss (who would remember nothing of the incident).[4] What seems certain is that *Conseiller culturel* Lévi-Strauss called in another man on a French cultural mission to the United States, architect Pierre-André Emery, knowing that he was a friend of Camus. Lévi-

Strauss asked Emery to go to the pier to meet Camus. Did Lévi-Strauss do this after being informed by Rubé and the others that Camus was held up at Immigration? In any case, Emery went down to the pier. When Camus emerged he was in a nervous state, told his Algiers friend that he had been questioned because he was carded as a Communist.[5] Still another friend was at the pier to greet him: the anti-Fascist Italian émigré writer Nicola Chiaromonte, who had spent the war years (since escaping with Camus' help from occupied France via Algeria and Morocco) writing for American periodicals such as *The New Republic*, *The Nation*, and *Partisan Review*. He now had an American wife, and Camus would be seeing much of Nicola and Miriam in New York.[6] A free man at last, Camus discovered that he was tired, and an attack of flu was returning; it was on unsteady feet that he walked his first blocks of Manhattan.

On the day following his arrival a press conference was held for the American and French press in the large salon of the French Cultural Services on Fifth Avenue. The guest was introduced by Lévi-Strauss. He would quickly express surprise at the abstract nature of the questions he was being asked. "And yet they had told me that America likes concrete questions," he observed. For the time being, he said when asked about his philosophic position, his philosophy consisted of doubts and uncertainties. "I'm too young to have a 'system'." He repeated, once again, his rejection of existentialism as a school à la mode and as a system.

Asked what he thought of the definition of the United States as the capital of materialistic civilization he replied: "Everywhere today man suffers from materialistic civilization. In poverty and hunger, European man is materialistic. Can it be otherwise?" He thought the real question was. Can man in his present plight act, nevertheless? He believed that the answer was yes. As for his own work, he explained (or so he was quoted), he had become a playwright by accident biographique, having had to earn his living as an actor (sic). His next work would be a novel about plague. To another question he replied that he had read American fiction from Dos Passos to Faulkner, and that he was certainly influenced by the interior technique of the American novel.

"But I wonder whether this technique doesn't lead to an impoverishment of the means of literary expression. Besides, American novelists are freeing themselves from this formula." He knew little about the American stage, apart from the work of Eugene O'Neill.

He was questioned about his resistance activity and replied that he preferred to speak of his comrades, for others had done far more than he had.

He had read and reread Kafka, whose work seemed to him prophetic, one of the most significant of our time. And the reporter for the New York French-language newspaper *La Victoire*, who signed "P.," perhaps for editor Michel P. Pobers, contributed the thought that Camus himself was "our Kafka without dreams."[7]

Camus' arrival in the United States had been anticipated by a full-page article in the *New York Herald Tribune Weekly Book Review* on March 24, under the headline:

BOLDEST WRITER IN FRANCE TODAY

In the article Justin O'Brien, of the Department of Romance Languages of Columbia University,

informed American readers (who had not yet
been able to read Camus unless they read French;
L'Etranger would appear in an English translation only in April) that Camus was "one of the
two or three most vivid young writers in France,
and his arrival in America this month is awaited
by many as one of the cultural events of the season." O'Brien went on: "Sartre has paved the
way for him; Vercors has praised his young
friend in New York, Chicago, and San Francisco;
our little reviews are beginning to mention his
name with something like reverence; Gênet [pen
name of Janet Flanner] made some swash comments in 'The New Yorker' on his popular play
now running in Paris." The article was certainly
the most thorough introduction of Camus that
would appear during his visit to New York.

On March 27, the third day of his stay in New
York, Camus was to have a significant encounter
in the person of A. J. Liebling, essayist-reporter for
The New Yorker—significant especially for Liebling, who would never forget his young French
friend, no more than he would forget anything
about the France he loved. Abbott Joseph Liebling, born in New York in 1904, had spent a year

at the Sorbonne and had covered the war from France, Great Britain, and North America from 1939 to 1944. He was awarded the French Legion of Honor, and three of his notable books were *The Road Back to Paris, Normandy Revisited*, and an anthology of resistance writing in French and English editions (*The Republic of Silence*, also published as *La République du silence*). Although The New Yorker's "Talk of the Town" interview with Camus, which appeared in that magazine on April 20, 1946, was unsigned, and the magazine's records contain no indication of who wrote it[8], in fact Liebling did, as he explained in the last article he was ever to write, a review of the American edition of Camus' journal, published in *The New Yorker* on February 8, 1964:

> When he first [sic] visited New York, shortly after the war, [Camus] was thirty-two, but I wrote that he reminded me of a character in the comic-strip "Harold Teen," an impression aided by his absurd suit, the product of a French tailor whose patterns evidently dated not only from before the war but from before the great crash of 1929. (His New York publisher, who was bringing out "The Stranger,"

hadn't offered him an advance on future work
and he had already spent his advance on "The
Stranger," so he was in no position to improve
his wardrobe.)

Liebling found Camus, "who is thirty-two and
dresses like a character in 'Harold Teen'," in a
hotel room on West Seventieth Street[9], described
him as having "a snub-nosed face that looks
more Spanish than French," noting Camus' an-
cestry (as Camus would have explained it to
Liebling: Spanish on his mother's side, Alsatian
on his father's). "His birth there gave him a dis-
tinctive chemistry, because the European cities
in French North Africa are as new and as ruth-
lessly commercial as Birmingham or Detroit." The
thing that bothered Camus about France, the
unidentified *New Yorker* interviewer remarked,
was the oversupply of historical and literary
associations. "What the heart craves, at certain
moments, is places without poetry," he quotes
Camus.* "West Seventieth Street ought to suit
him fine," "Talk of the Town" concluded.

* In Le Minotaure ou la Halte d'Oran: "Ce que le coeur demande à
certains moments ... ce sont justement des lieux sans poésie."

A student of journalism as well as a passionate admirer of things French, Liebling was of course interested in the journalist Camus. The interview opened with Camus' "idea for a daily newspaper which would take a lot of the fun out of newspapering." Camus told him: "It would be a critical newspaper, to be published one hour after the first editions of the other papers, twice a day, morning and evening. It would evaluate the probable element of truth in the other papers' main stories, with due regard to editorial policies and the past performances of the correspondents. Once equipped with card-indexed dossiers on the correspondents, a critical newspaper could work very fast. After a few weeks the whole tone of the press would conform more closely to reality. An international service." The interviewer also reported that *Caligula* had been acquired for New York production. Summing up Camus' work and philosophy, and the symbol of Sisyphus condemned to pushing a rock up a hill, "Talk of the Town" observed that "For a man arrived at such a grim conclusion, M. Camus seemed unduly cheerful, as did, in fact, M. Sartre when he was here some weeks ago." "Just because you have pessimistic thoughts, you don't have to *act* pessimistic," Camus is quoted. "One has to pass the time somehow. Look at Don Juan."

On March 28, Camus was to make his most important public appearance in the United States; in the company of two other writers born of the French resistance, he would speak at the McMillin Theater on the campus of Columbia University. The chairman of the sponsoring committee, Justin O'Brien, had discussed the meeting on the previous day with the guest speakers in what O'Brien later remembered as "Camus' room in one of those mothy hotels on upper Broadway." The other speakers would be Vercors, pseudonym of Jean Bruller, whose *Le Silence de la mer*, published in France by an underground printer, had already appeared in English, and Thimerais (Léon Motchane), not known in America because the essay he had published at the clandestine Editions de Minuit had not yet reached American shores. O'Brien later noted "the utter simplicity" of Camus' smile, "reminiscent of a Paris street urchin." Camus was the youngest of the group, and received an admiring glance from an attractive girl who rode up with them in the elevator.

Then the moment they were in Camus' room "the athletic young man had stretched out on the bed with a few notes in front of him" and "easily dominated the group."

That is how it looked to O'Brien, but in fact Camus would spend the following whole day writing his talk, and when he confronted the crowd at the McMillin Theater he would experience a quiver of stage fright. For there were at least 1,200 persons in the hall that evening (no one could recall any meeting in French that had drawn an audience of more than three hundred in New York). And Camus—O'Brien's recollection again—clearly dominated that audience. "Making no distinctions between victors and vanquished in the war, he rapidly sketched a horridly debased conception of man that was, he said, the legacy of World War II.... When he told us that, as human beings of the twentieth century, we were all of us responsible for the war, and even for the horrors we had just been fighting ... all of us in the huge hall were convinced, I think, of our common culpability. Then Camus ... told us how we could contribute, even in the humblest way, to re-establishing the honesty and dignity of men."[10]

The original French text of Camus' talk, entitled "The Human Crisis" (perhaps this is a re-translation of the subject of the evening's symposium, "The Crisis of Mankind") has not been found, but an English translation exists and has been published.[11]

Camus began by suggesting that he had not reached the proper age for lecturing, but he had been told that the important thing was not to express his personal views but to present elementary facts about France. He had chosen to speak not of literature or theater but of the spiritual experience of the men of his generation, of men "born just before or during the first great war, [who] reached adolescence during the world economic crisis, and were twenty the year Hitler took power. To complete their education they were then provided with the war in Spain, Munich, the war of 1939, the defeat, and four years of occupation and secret struggle." He illustrated the human crisis with four stories. In an apartment rented by the Gestapo a concierge proceeds to set the place in order, oblivious of two persons still bleeding and tightly bound. To the reproaches of one of the torture victims she replies: "I never pay attention to what my tenants do." (The story has already been remarked in Camus' journal.)

A German officer interrogates one of Camus' comrades in Lyons. In a previous session the prisoner's ears had been torn to shreds, and the German asks in a tone of affection or of solicitude: "How are your ears now?" In Greece, a woman is asked by a German officer to choose which of her three sons taken as hostage should be spared; she chooses the eldest because he has a family, thereby condemning the two others as the German officer intended. A group of deported women, among whom is a comrade of Camus, is repatriated to France via Switzerland. Seeing a funeral, they laugh hysterically: "So that is how the dead are treated *here*." (Also taken from his journal.)

These stories allow him to affirm that there is a human crisis since the death or the torture of a human being can, in our world, be examined with indifference, with friendly or experimental interest, or without any response at all. He summed up what was wrong in "the single tendency described as the cult of efficiency and of abstraction." The problem was Hegel's "detestable principle" that man is made for history. Anything which serves history is considered good; acts are justified not as good or bad but by their effectiveness. Men of his generation were tempted into thinking nothing was true, or that historical fate is the only truth. Their revolt was to say no to the absurdity of the world, to abstractions, affirming nevertheless that there was something in us which rejected the offense and which could not be endlessly humiliated.

What must we do? Camus asked. "We must call things by their right names and realize that we kill millions of men each time we permit ourselves to think certain thoughts." We must rid the world of terror, put politics back in its rightful place, a secondary one, move from negation to positive values, to universalism. "There is in France and in Europe today a generation which takes the view that whoever puts his trust in the human condition is a madman, while whoever despairs of events is a coward.... Whenever one judges France or any other country or question in terms of power, one aids and sustains a conception of man which logically leads to his mutilation...."

One of O'Brien's students passed a note up to the stage to inform the chairman that thieves had just stolen the evening's receipts, which had been intended for French war orphans. After Camus finished his talk O'Brien took the floor to observe that the "Crisis of Mankind" was at their very door. Someone rose from the audience to suggest that on their way out everyone pay his entrance fee a second time, and the two girls whose cash box had been stolen set up the box again. The second "take" amounted to more than the original one, an effect of Camus' "persuasive words," thought O'Brien. One of the speakers told the incident to *Le Figaro*, providing an opportunity for a story about America's gangsters and generous hearts.[10] Camus himself was enthralled by the event, seeing it as the embodiment of American crime.[2]

The French-language weekly *La Victoire* of April 6 hailed the evening at Columbia as *"Une grande fête française,"* assuring its readers that the meeting would occupy a place of its own in the annals of the French colony of the United States. (The article contained some choice lines from the original French of Camus' talk, all that seem to have survived.) Was there a question period after the talks? An employee of the French Cultural Services recalled a question from the audience: "How many Frenchmen were there in the resistance?" and Camus' quick reply, a figure like 360,728—an ironic way to suggest that in such situations numbers didn't count.[12]

Camus did submit to a question-and-answer session at Columbia, in any case, at the Maison Française. Camus had telephoned its director, Eugene Sheffer, at the suggestion of a former student of Sheffer's, Peter Rhodes, onetime United Press correspondent and chief of the Psychological Warfare Branch of the Office of War Information in Paris, to say that he would like to meet American students. Sheffer set up the meeting in the salon of the Maison Française, invited some fifty Columbia undergraduates and a few of his fellow teachers. Camus walked in, and his boyish grin put them all at ease at once. He asked his listeners to sit on the floor, and then he proceeded to ask questions. Camus said that he had visited several European capitals where men would stare at women on the street, but it didn't seem to happen in New York and he wanted to know why. The question was greeted by embarrassed silence until a professor, Otis Fellows, broke in with: "Monsieur Camus, in this country we believe that there is a time and a place for everything." Camus stared at Fellows for a moment in surprise and then broke into a hearty laugh, acknowledging that it was a very good answer indeed, but one which had never occurred to him.[13]

His friend Emery arranged for Camus to be received at the home of Dr. Ludwig Eidelberg and his wife Marthe, who as a young widow of French birth had met Eidelberg in 1938. He had been head of the Neurological Clinic in Vienna, had taught at the Viennese Psychoanalytical Institute, and was one of the psychoanalysts whose evacuation from Nazi-controlled Austria had been facilitated by British and American colleagues. He was practicing at Oxford when Marthe met him in Paris. After their marriage they moved to the United States, where Dr. Eidelberg developed a practice while teaching at the Psychoanalytic Institute. Later he would publish the first *Encyclopedia of Psychoanalysis*; he died in 1971.

The Eidelbergs were living in a small apartment on East Eighty-sixth Street with a view over Central Park's reservoir and toward the George Washington Bridge. There were fewer than a dozen guests for dinner. Mrs. Eidelberg realized that she was being an inadequate hostess, because she talked to Camus all evening long. Having been in exile for seven years, she felt uprooted, and here she was seated beside a fellow Frenchman, and a great writer and resistance hero in the bargain. Emery had found a copy of *Lettres à un ami allemand* in a secondhand bookshop, and Camus autographed it for her:

...because we have many common passions...

Emery had also brought along a phonograph record containing a text by Camus on the liberation of Paris, but it was read disappointingly by an effeminate male voice. Although quite taken with his hostess, Camus found time to speak with her husband, discussing psychoanalysis and Caligula, even displaying familiarity with a little-known paper on that Roman emperor written by a Viennese psychoanalyst. Camus told Mrs. Eidelberg that he found New York overpowering;

when all the lights went on in the evening the city seemed to be on fire—a frightening experience for him.[14]

Some days later Marthe Eidelberg accompanied him to a cocktail party given in his honor at the Institut Français on East Sixtieth Street (now called French Institute-Alliance Française). While she knew that many of the French settled in the United States had been anti-Free French, partisans either of Pétain or of General Giraud, at the party everyone wished to shake hands with the guest of honor, for of course they had all been patriots. Whenever Mrs. Eidelberg noticed someone with a reputation as a notorious Vichyite, she would whisper to Camus: "He's a scoundrel!" They had a wonderful time.[15] Presumably this party was held in conjunction with a talk that Camus gave at the institute on "Le Théâtre à Paris aujourd'hui." Nothing remains of the talk except the institute's log, which recorded that there were 294 persons in the audience and the weather was fair; weather was always mentioned in the log because it had an effect on attendance. The capacity of the hall was about three hundred.[16] Camus also visited New York's Lycée

Français, where he chatted with students on their own level, answered questions. He also talked with Pierre Brodet, then a teacher there, and autographed a copy of *L'Etranger* for him.[17]

Early in his stay Camus was able to move out of the mothy hotel and into a small duplex apartment in a twin-tower high-rise standing on Central Park West between Sixty-second and Sixty-third streets, a 1930s streamline-style building called Century Apartments, and he got it without having any rent to pay. His benefactor was a furrier named Zaharo, believed to be of Polish extraction; his illiterate immigrant father had grown rich in furs. Apparently Zaharo had heard Camus speak and was enthralled, and phoned Camus' hotel to tell him that he was leaving town on business, begging him to take his apartment. At first Camus refused, and Zaharo asked if he could telephone occasionally to see if Camus would change his mind. Then Camus caught cold and when Zaharo called again he accepted. Camus told his wife one story of Zaharo's he remembered. Zaharo's father had become blind, and his son would read to him. One day the son read Plato's account of the death of Socrates and the father said: "From now on you will read me this until the day I die," and the son complied.[18]

The apartment was by no means an elegant one. It consisted of a living room and a kitchen on one level, a small bedroom or two and a bath upstairs. Camus would have an American breakfast at the corner drugstore: orange juice, two eggs and bacon, toast and coffee.[19]

Soon Camus had created his own nucleus of friends and drinking or at least walking companions in New York. He remained in close touch with Pierre Rubé, and when he felt a fever rising— as happened occasionally—he would phone the doctor for reassurance. Rubé observed that Camus liked or needed constant companionship, whether of men or of women. They went together to cheap restaurants and cafeterias, to a Harlem dance hall to listen to jazz. Clearly Camus was feeling very alone in this city so unlike anything he had ever known. Rubé also observed that men a bit older than Camus, like himself, always felt fatherly toward Camus, and women felt motherly. Camus expressed astonishment at the beauty of American women, but also experienced what he called their terrifying in-accessibility, and Rubé himself knew of cases where Frenchmen had become impotent with American women, for they confessed to him after-wards. It was in the Bowery, where the women were old and ravaged, that Camus relaxed notice-ably.[2] Even Claude Lévi-Strauss, who saw very little of Camus during the latter's nearly three-month visit, once took Camus to dinner in China-town, then to a brassy cabaret in the Bowery spe-cializing in women singers who were not young, "in general grotesque and of a repulsive aspect."[4] Was it then Lévi-Strauss who introduced Camus to Sammy's Bowery Follies (then a popular caba-ret answering to this description)? The notion is pleasant.

One evening Pierre Rubé and Camus went to pick up A. J. Liebling at *The New Yorker*. Liebling took them to Little Italy to look into shop win-dows displaying elegant bridal gowns, so incon-gruous on these grim streets. Liebling led them on from bar to bar, although Camus was careful about his drinking because of his ever fragile health. Their escort then showed them the Bowery, ushered them into bars to hear third-rate singers. Was it rather Liebling who introduced Camus to this scene which so fascinated him? By the end of the evening Liebling was quite drunk, but his two companions managed to get him into a taxi and gave the driver his home address.[2] Camus later told a Paris friend how he had loved Liebling at first sight.

One night, Camus would recall, they staged a drinking contest which Camus won (but that is inconsistent with Dr. Rubé's observation on his friend's cautious behavior). Liebling amused Camus with a story of how he had invented a boxer whom he reported on regularly in *The New Yorker*.[20] The Camus-Liebling friendship would be carried on under similarly rowdy circumstances during the American writer's visits to France. And in the last days of Liebling's life, in delirium, before he went into his final coma, he spoke only in French and was apparently addressing his friend Camus. But Camus had died by that time. In the spring of Liebling's final year, 1963, he traveled to North Africa in the hope of alleviating a deep depression that had settled over him; his wife saw it as a search for Camus.[21]

Liebling once observed comically about his friend: "His energies were dissipated in creative writing and we lost a great journalist."[22]

One day Camus even asked Eugene Sheffer of the Maison Française to accompany him to Sammy's Bowery Follies; Sheffer remembered Camus saying that his curiosity had been aroused by advertising for the establishment. Was Sheffer then the witness to Camus' introduction to the *Walpurgisnacht* of lower Manhattan? Sheffer recalled an incredible show in which all of the actresses were so-called former burlesque queens now well along in middle age. As he watched these faded, overweight women go through their bumps and grinds, he felt it was both a hilarious and somewhat degrading performance, and he noticed that Camus got a great kick out of it.[13] What Camus *was* feeling, as he told his journal, was that here at last was the concrete.

Camus tried to put some order into the disorder of his impressions of this city which reminded him of Oran, impressions he was picking up in the ways we have just observed. He put much of what he saw and felt into long and funny letters to the Michel Gallimards, letters which he knew would also be read by his wife, who was then "camping" in their apartment at the top of the Gallimard town house on the Rue de l'Université. And then when he got home he borrowed the letters and made of them an essay he called "Pluies de New York"[23] published in the Pléiade edition of his work. (The chief source of the essay was the letter he wrote the Gallimards on April 20, and which he signed "Al Capone"; his letters to Michel and Janine usually bore comical salutations and occasionally comical signatures.) Since he wrote these impressions first of all for friends and family, they can be taken as the closest approximation to what he really felt at the time; since they are available in extant publications in both French and English, they need not be repeated, and only (for the sake of thoroughness) the reference to the Bowery Follies will be cited:

> I knew what was waiting for me, these nights on the Bowery, where at a few steps from those splendid shops with wedding dresses (not one of the wax brides was smiling), some 500 yards of such shops, live forgotten men, men who let themselves be poor in the city of bankers.

It is the city's most sinister neighborhood, where one doesn't meet any women, where one man in three is drunk, and where in a curious café, seemingly out of a Western movie, one can see fat old actresses who sing of ruined lives and maternal love, stamping their feet at the refrain, and shaking spasmodically, to the roaring of the audience, the packets of shapeless flesh with which age had covered them. Another old woman plays the drums, and she resembles an owl, and some evenings one feels like knowing her life story, at one of those rare moments when geography disappears, and when solitude becomes a somewhat disordered truth.

And perhaps one might linger over this essay to savor the nice things Camus had to say about New York, about which he said he still knew nothing, although he had "powerful and fugitive emotions, an impatient nostalgia, instants of heartbreak." He loved the mornings and the nights of New York.

After the lecture at the French Institute on April 16, a young woman seated with her mother in the audience was introduced to Camus. Her name was Patricia Blake, she had completed her college program at Smith (although she would not receive her diploma until June), and she was working for Vogue magazine, writing for the *New York Times Book Review*. She was nineteen years old and stunning. That, and the fact that she was intelligent and spoke good French, made her the most desirable possible companion for the tourist Albert Camus. He lost no time in making a date with her (for the very next day). Although she had to spend days at her job, they could have lunch together, and evenings they would go sightseeing, to meet friends, or just walking; she also accompanied him to his lectures. He had brought his draft of *La Peste*, and she typed part of it for him while he was in New York. There was also time for serious talking, and she allowed herself to be persuaded to change her politics: She had been sympathetic to Communism, and his description of the crimes of Stalinism made her feel differently about the Soviet Union. (Patricia Blake was later to become an authority on the Soviet Union and things Communist.) After Camus' return to France the relationship was pursued in correspondence and when Patricia

Blake would visit France; for a while she lived in Paris when she was married to the composer Nicolas Nabokov.

She was also concerned for Camus, for she was observing a side of him that he managed to hide from his public: He ran a fever every day in New York. If he felt very ill he would ask her to leave him; that happened four or five times. (She felt that he was coughing up blood but she could not be certain of it.) His attitude toward the future seemed that of a man who did not expect to live a long time. He never explicitly told her that his illness could be fatal but she felt that it must be. She knew that he was seeing a doctor although she did not know who it was. (But she did accompany Camus on his outings with Pierre Rubé.)

His talk about life was cynical; it took on the form of black humor. He told deathbed jokes, e.g., the last words of the writer Alfred Jarry, while friends leaned over his hospital bed. Finally he said, "A toothpick," and died. And when Ingres was dying his wife called in a priest, although the painter had been an atheist all his life. The priest told him: "You will soon be in the face of

God." Ingres: "Always in the face, never in pro-
file." Camus was fascinated by funeral services
in New York and asked Patricia Blake to buy him
undertakers' journals, one of which was called
Sunnyside.

She was to discover that he loved much New
York lore: Chinatown, the Bowery, popular dance
halls, garish and gawdy night clubs with floor
shows. Although his understanding of spoken
English was slight, he would ask his young companion to listen to conversations at adjoining
restaurant tables and repeat them to him. (If he
could not carry off a conversation in English, he
could read the language, and would sometimes
write her a few lines in English.) They would go
to restaurants like Le Steak Pommes Frites or
Larré's, went to the theater a great deal (while
the Old Vic was visiting New York with Laurence
Olivier, they saw Sheridan's *The Critic* and Soph-
ocles' *Oedipus Rex* on the same bill). Camus did-
n't seem to care for music, so they attended no
concerts, but they did go to the Chinese opera,
which was then housed in the foundations of a
lower Manhattan bridge, where Camus was fascinated by the stagehands who walked onto the

stage during the performance to change the scenery. They would try different restaurants in China-town. (Patricia Blake would later write an article about Chinatown, and one of the first surveys of the American "death industry," about which she became interested through Camus, for *Life* magazine.) Then they would go to Grand Street, where he would look at the rows of shops displaying wedding dresses (which he presumably saw first with Liebling).

Camus liked the Central Park Zoo and was an indefatigable visitor; Blake may have seen it with him twenty times. They would walk across the park from the Century Apartments, often in the afternoon, occasionally in the evening. Camus enjoyed observing the monkeys.

She discovered that he had a phobia about going into stores, and she would walk in to make purchases for him. (This led to a misunderstanding: Once, when Pierre Rubé was walking downtown with Camus and Blake, they stopped at the window of a chocolate shop, perhaps on Fifty-seventh Street, and Rubé heard Camus ask the young woman to go inside to buy the chocolates he was pointing to. Rubé assumed that this was an example of Camus' sovereign attitude toward women,[2] when in fact it was an example of the phobia Blake had already witnessed.)

Camus was accompanied by his young admirer to meet people he had to see in New York, such as the writer Pierre de Lanux, who drove Camus to Fort Tryon Park for the view, and then to New Jersey, where they admired the East Orange Public Library and its large children's reading room until Camus noticed that the library's card index under "Philosophy" listed William James and no one else. They met publisher Jacques Schiffrin, who had been a friend of Gide (about whom Camus made a derisive remark which brought on laughter, but Blake didn't know whether or not Camus was joking about his lack of appreciation of Gide's talents). Camus had met the Thomist philosopher Etienne Gilson and they spent an evening with him. After dinner they went to a noisy night club where she fainted and Gilson seemed, to say the least, out of his element. She went with Camus to the NBC studios for an interview of Camus by George Day, beamed to France on April 27.[24]

Day had begun the interview by saying that

he did not desire polite stereotyped phrases but wished Camus' impressions of "our country." Camus replied that indeed he could give impressions but not judgments, because it was difficult to judge a nation which required six days to cross from coast to coast. As for details, they could have no significance in themselves. He noted that garbage collectors wore gloves, that brides in shop windows look sad, while advertising is all smiles.

As for general judgments: Camus said that he had come to the United States as other Europeans had, with the vague hope that a formula or life style then being sought in Europe could be found there. He couldn't be definitive about what he had discovered. Were Americans interested in French culture? Yes, if the curiosity expressed by students in the universities, and if their theses and examination subjects were indicative.

While the demands, problems, and confusions of American and French youth were similar, American young people did not seem ready to change things, probably because they lived in a more stable society, an advantage for them, although for Frenchmen who needed to feel less alone it could not seem an advantage. Was it a lack of dynamism? Certainly not, Camus told his interviewer and his French radio audience. He was impressed with the vigor and the sturdiness of young Americans, struck by the fact that there was no sign of ruse in their expressions, and when you come from Europe that was important.

What young Americans lacked most, Camus told Day, was passion in the sense he understood it, passion for justice, for example. The French may have this passion because recent events required it of them, and he agreed with Day finally that Americans could be as passionate for justice as the French. Day suggested that traditional Anglo-Saxon reserve explained the absence of visible excitement.[25]

The first out-of-town campus visit was to Vassar, on April 6, where he discovered a legion of long-legged starlets decorating the lawns. The college's *Vassar Miscellany News* of April 3 had described Camus' visit to the United States as "one of the cultural events of the season"—the phrase perhaps taken from Justin O'Brien in the *Herald Tribune*. Camus spoke on "La Théâtre français d'aujourd'hui" at Avery Hall under the auspices of the Department of French and the French Club. When Sartre had been in New York, he had declined a visit to Vassar but said that Camus would come, so when she heard he was on his way Mrs. Maria Tastevin-Miller, then chairman of the Department of French, asked the French Consulate in New York to request Camus' appearance. He took a train to Pough-keepsie, and told Mrs. Tastevin-Miller that he was very impressed with the student body, es-pecially with her French speakers; he spoke to the audience in French without an interpreter.[26] On April 15 he spoke on "La Crise de l'homme," this time at the New School for Social Research in Manhattan; on April 16 he made the capital acquaintance of Patricia Blake after his talk at the Institut Français; and on April 29 he spoke at Pendleton Hall at Wellesley, where the sub-ject was announced as "Littérature française d'aujourd'hui."[27]

At Bryn Mawr he stayed at the home of Ger-maine Brée, who happened to be a childhood-friend of the Faures of Oran; later she would be-come an authority on Camus' writing. He spoke informally to the students, his general theme being how to cope with contemporary problems without embracing a metaphysics or a system.[28] Either at the same meeting or at another session with students at the college he discussed the war and its effect on French writers just beginning to be known in the United States. Someone asked why he had left the existentialist movement and he replied impatiently that he was not an existentialist. He described his divergences with Sartre, talked movingly about Dostoevsky. Someone asked him what he thought of Proust now, and he answered something like "not much." A member of the audience noticed that he smoked incessantly. Patricia Blake joined him for the day, and they traveled back to New York by train after a further talk given in a large auditorium in Philadelphia (whose sponsorship and audience have not been traced).[24]

Back in New York, he spoke at Brooklyn College. It was a special occasion: The school was inaugurating its second Journée Française. Before Camus' talk President Harry D. Gideonse made a brief speech on France, a student recited Paul Eluard's hymn to freedom. Camus gave the student audience his impressions of the American youth he had been meeting on various campuses, for this was to be the final stop on his tour of Eastern universities. He said that he thought youth was the same everywhere in the world. But he had expected to find American youth more passionate. Inertia is man's greatest temptation. It is not enough to do one's job; youth must be active in the world, for the world would be saved by this generation or it would not be saved. He described a "solidarity of misfortune": If we accept the power principle then we must struggle. Concerning European pessimism (life is tragedy) and American optimism (life is marvelous), he felt that a synthesis was necessary. "We must create, on the level of sensibility, the United States of the world that we are incapable of founding on the juridical level." He appealed for material help for French students, but also for exchanges of correspondence and then of persons.

After the talk he replied to questions. Once more he was asked if he was an existentialist. He said he was not, because existentialism claims to answer all questions, which is impossible for a single philosophy, and he wanted the freedom to say yes as well as no. The meeting ended with a piano solo of music by Debussy.[29]

He had time for a visit to Washington, D.C. Here, and along Riverside Drive in Manhattan, from the top of the Hotel Plaza overlooking Central Park, he was inspired to reveries by a peculiarly American landscape, where crowds seemed not to spoil a certain softness and lack of tension he found in this country.[30] He had two days on the beach at Falmouth on Cape Cod, where he discovered lobster Newburg. He met and talked with more people he admired and with whom he could relate, such as Waldo Frank, who he felt was one of the rare superior men he had met in the United States. He visited the Chiaromontes at their West Eighth Street Greenwich Village apartment, met personalities such as the writer and critic Lionel Abel there.[6] He was spotted at a soirée at William Phillips', co-founder of *Partisan Review*, on West Eleventh Street, in an apartment described as an informal salon, a home away from home for New York's intellectuals;[31] perhaps Chiaromonte brought him there.

On the lighter side, he teamed up with Jac-

ques Schoeller, the brother of Guy, Michel Gallimard's friend. He had been an early employee of
Gaston Gallimard at Publications Zed, producing
trashy magazines such as *Detective*, and later set
up an advertising agency for Gallimard. During
the war he escaped from a prison camp and from
North Africa went to Mexico, where he founded
a radio station. He knew New York well, and took
Camus around on foot. They saw Harlem, Coney
Island, and Brooklyn, the West Side Highway,
night clubs, the old skating rink on Fifty-second
Street where organ music accompanied the ska-
ters' acrobatics. Schoeller found Camus naïve
and shy, with little experience of the wide world.
His candor seemed almost childlike, he was not
entirely sure of himself. And whenever Camus
wasn't busy with Patricia Blake or with cultural
obligations, he would phone Schoeller; they
would arrange to meet at the end of a reception
or other social encounter, and then go out on the
town.[32]

On April 11 the firm of Alfred A. Knopf pub-
lished *L'Etranger* in an English translation by
Stuart Gilbert. It was greeted in that day's New
York *Times* in a review by Charles Poore, who

called *The Stranger* "a novel of crime and punish-
ment" which "should touch off in this country a
renewed burst of discussion about the young
French writers who are at the moment making
more unusual literary news than the writers of
any other country." Despite what he felt to be
the "Britannic" quality of Gilbert's translation,
the reviewer pronounced Camus' novel "brilliant-
ly told." The book and the author were naturals
for Knopf, who had pioneered in modern European literature, and Alfred Knopf's wife and best
talent scout, Blanche, had met Camus in Paris
almost a year earlier, and would be meeting him
there again and again on her trips to the Conti-
nent.[33] Knopf threw a party for Camus on the old
Astor Roof above Times Square.[34] *The New
Yorker*'s "Talk of the Town" interview appeared
shortly thereafter: the Sunday New York *Times
Book Review* had already published a report
from John L. Brown in Paris identifying Camus
as an outstanding leader among writers who had
emerged in France since the war. Then in *The
New Republic* of April 29 Chiaromonte reviewed
the American edition of *L'Etranger* in the form
of a lengthy introduction to Camus the man and

the writer; the novel was described as "admirable."

Camus received consecration of sorts in the June 1 *Vogue*, which published a somewhat coy full-page head portrait of him by the photographer Cecil Beaton, over a caption which described Camus as a "slight, thirty-two-year-old Frenchman." If *Vogue* saw Camus as slight, it may have been that in America he did seem slight; Beaton himself was over six feet tall. Camus was extremely thin at the time, often seemed tired and sickly. His clothes didn't fit him properly—they were baggy, and this too would have contributed to the impression.[24] He was nevertheless taken by the ladies of *Vogue* for a young Humphrey Bogart, an observation which delighted him.[23]

Then the New York *Post* opened its magazine section on June 5 with a full-page interview by Dorothy Norman, who reported that "As France's most talented young writer to emerge from the 'resistance' period, he has had a warm welcome from many in this country." She noted his shudder when asked whether he was an existentialist. "You can explain nothing by way of principles and ideologies," he declared. He felt that "revolt" usually implied romantic revolt à la Byron or a form of Marxism. "But revolt can be much more modest in its implications." He gave the example of the hero of *L'Etranger*, "a man who refuses to lie.... If a man dares to say what he truly feels, if he revolts against having to lie, then society will destroy him in the end." The interviewer found Camus modest in his comments, including his impressions of New York, where once again he explained that he was moved not by skyscrapers but by the Bowery. He preferred Melville and Henry James to any twentieth-century writers. He dressed and spoke in a relaxed way (tweed; no jargon). If he was struck by the fact that he could wander around the United States without identity papers, the American attitude to Negroes disturbed him. He had expressed his own feelings, he noted, by seeing to it that the works of Richard Wright were translated and published in Paris. He felt that Europe could offer something to America, a sense of disquiet.

Outlining his future, he described the completed cycle of books on absurdity, and that to come on revolt. Finally there would be a novel,

essay, and play based on the concept "we are."
What then? "Then," he said with a smile, "there
will be a fourth phase in which I shall write a
book about love." He had given up journalism in
order to devote himself to writing, but it was not
easy to support a wife and two children that way
in present-day France, especially when he
refused to compromise or to popularize.

While in New York, Camus had one serious
piece of work to do for his friends at Gallimard.
The French publisher had a contract with An-
toine de Saint-Exupéry signed in 1929 which gave
it all rights to his future work (at that time, and
until a French law of 1957 barred such agreements,
publishers could obtain such an option on an
author's future work), but when Saint-Exupéry
came to the United States in 1938 he had signed a
contract with an American publisher, Reynal &
Hitchcock, for *Wind, Sand and Stars*, and during the occupation of France had written and
published with Reynal & Hitchcock *Flight to
Arras* and *The Little Prince*. Now Saint-Exupéry
was dead, and Gallimard filed suit in New York
against the American house.[35] Gaston Gallimard's
brother Raymond, Michel's father, came to New

York to follow the proceedings, and was roundly attacked in the New York French-language weekly *La Victoire*:

> Is he coming to pursue the ridiculous and scandalous law suits against American publishers who committed the crime of helping French authors during the somber years of the occupation [of France] ... while the NRF had Drieu La Rochelle as its Fuehrer? Is he coming, on the contrary, to put an end to a policy which discredits all of French publishing?

Saint-Exupéry's widow, then living in New York, had asked the French-language press not to speak of the matter until the Gallimards had arrived in New York, and now the press was anxious to know more.[36] Camus served mainly as an intermediary, meeting the widow, providing moral support to Raymond Gallimard. He was convinced of the moral right of the Gallimards, of the low state of U.S. publishing, especially of French writers during the war—or at least this was the argument he used to appease the Gallimards.[23] The suit ended without bloodshed, with a court order providing some satisfaction to each side.

The American stage adaptation of *Caligula* was to be done by a young producer named Harald Bromley, although the project would never get off the ground. Nevertheless Camus was impressed by this sympathetic and enterprising young man. When it was time for him to fulfill his lecture commitment in French Canada at the end of May, Bromley offered to drive him there, and even bought a secondhand car for the trip.[2] They left New York on May 25 to drive up through the Adirondacks, stopped at a mountain inn at what seemed a remote part of that region (at Camp Downey, Clayburg, New York); for a brief moment Camus imagined himself, in the face of the silence of nature, the simplicity of the lodgings, the remoteness, staying here forever—cutting ties with the world as he knew it.[30]

They arrived in Montreal on May 26. But this time Camus had really had enough, and he was anxious to return to France. He had even tried to change his Montreal lecture date, but the Canadians replied that you can postpone a lecture, you can't advance its date. He had no good things to say about this Canadian experience, although on the whole he was satisfied with his transatlantic trip. It had been useful to him; he had even discovered that he was not a bad public speaker. Physically he was in better shape than he had been for a long time; with hot baths and vitamins he had gained some weight. But it was time to go home now.[23]

He remembered to arrange for shipment to his family of a food parcel—in fact a crate weighing 176 pounds and containing six pounds of sugar, six pounds of coffee, three pounds of powdered eggs, six pounds of flour, four pounds of rice, six pounds of chocolate, thirty pounds of baby food, twenty-eight pounds of soap, and other products, not to speak of some $160 in purchases which accompanied him. On June 21, after ten days at sea, he was in Bordeaux, where his wife and the Michel Gallimards were waiting for him, and they drove back to Paris in Michel Gallimard's automobile.[3]

On shipboard his old travel sadness had settled in again. He had time to think about what was in store for him on his return.

> In 25 years I shall be 57 [he told his journal].
> Thus 25 years to create my work and to find

what I seek. Then, old age and death. I know what is most important for me. And I still find the way to yield to small temptations, to waste time in vain conversation or sterile strolling. I have mastered two or three things in me. But how far I am from that superiority which I need so badly.[30]

Notes

1. Quoted in the Pléiade edition of Camus' work.

2. Dr. Pierre Rubé.

3. Madame Albert Camus.

4. Claude Lévi-Strauss.

5. Pierre-André Emery.

6. Miriam Chiaromonte.

7. *La Victoire* (New York), March 30, 1946. After May 11 this weekly merged with *France-Amérique*.

8. Raymond Sokolov.

9. In this article in the April 20 *New Yorker*, Liebling spoke of Camus' "first five days in America," suggesting that the interview took place on March 29 or 30, not at their first meeting on March 27. This is consistent with the recollection of Professor Pierre Guédenet, then deputy cultural conseiller of the French Embassy, who had asked Liebling to be a sponsor of the March 28 Columbia University evening. Liebling was introduced to Camus prior to that meeting. Then, when Liebling told Guédenet that he would like to see Camus again, Guédenet set up a meeting at his apartment on Gramercy Park. Professor Pierre Guédenet. The interview took place at the West Seventieth Street hotel. Which hotel? Most probably it was the Embassy, at Broadway and Seventieth Street. Nearby the Sherman Square

Hotel and the Ansonia were popular with artists and writers, but there is no reason to believe that Camus stayed in either of these.

10. Justin O'Brien, "Albert Camus, Militant," in *The Columbia University Forum Anthology*, ed. by Peter Spackman and Lee Ambrose (New York, 1968), also published in O'Brien, *The French Literary Horizon* (New Brunswick, N.J., 1967); an abridged version in French appeared in *Hommage à Albert Camus*.

11. In *Twice a Year* (New York), Fall-Winter 1946-47, and in *Revue des Lettres Modernes* (Paris), Nos. 315-322, 1972.

12. Anne Minor-Gavronsky.

13. Eugene Sheffer.

14. Marthe Eidelberg; Pierre-André Emery.

15. Marthe Eidelberg.

16. Jean Vallier, director, French Institute.

17. Pierre Brodet.

18. Madame Albert Camus.

19. Patricia Blake; Janine Gallimard.

20. Jean Daniel.

21. Mrs. A. J. Liebling (Jean Stafford).

22. A. J. Liebling, *The Press* (New York, 1961).

23. Janine Gallimard.

24. Patricia Blake.

25. Partial recording, courtesy of Patricia Blake.

26. Maria Tastevin-Miller. Mrs. Tastevin-Miller remembers the subject of the talk as "The Crisis of Mankind" (La Crise de l'homme), so perhaps Camus did not follow the original program.

27. *Wellesley News*, April 25, 1946; Professor George Stambolian; Germaine Brée. Pierre-André Emery recalls that Camus was the victim of heckling at the New School when he said that the October [Russian] Revolution cost too much in human lives.

28. Patricia Blake; Germaine Brée.

29. *France-Amérique* (New York), May 19, 1946. Files of the French-American press were consulted at the French Cultural Services, New York.

30. This and other personal observations by Camus were recorded in his notebooks, published as *Journaux de voyage* (Paris, 1978).

31. In Susan Edminston and Linda D. Cirino, *Literary New York* (Boston, 1976).

32. Jacques Schoeller.

33. Blanche Knopf, "Albert Camus in the *Sun*," in *Atlantic Monthly* (Boston), February 1961.

34. Alfred A. Knopf.

35. *Publishers' Weekly* (New York), April 13, 1946.

36. *La Victoire* (New York), April 13, 1946.